W9-DEW-047

Foxes

Foxes

Mary Ann McDonald

T H E   C H I L D ' S   W O R L D®, INC.

Library of Congress Cataloging-in-Publication Data
McDonald, Mary Ann.
Foxes / by Mary Ann McDonald.
p.   cm.
Includes index.
Summary: Describes the physical characteristics,
behavior, and habitat of foxes.
ISBN 1-56766-479-2 (lib. reinforced : alk. paper)
1. Foxes—Juvenile literature.   [1. Foxes.]   I. Title
QL737.C22M383   1998
599.775—dc21   97-38096
CIP
AC

Photo Credits

© 1997 Bruce Montagne/Dembinsky Photo Assoc. Inc.: 23
© Darrell Gulin/Dembinsky Photo Assoc. Inc.: cover, 10
© 1995 Dominique Braud/Dembinsky Photo Assoc. Inc.: 26
© DPA/Dembinsky Photo Assoc. Inc.: 15
© Gary Meszaros/Dembinsky Photo Assoc. Inc.: 19, 30
© 1997 Jim Roetzel/Dembinsky Photo Assoc. Inc.: 9, 13
© Joe McDonald: 2, 6, 20
© 1993 Mark. J. Thomas/Dembinsky Photo Assoc. Inc.: 24
© Mary Ann McDonald: 29
© 1997 Russ Gutshall/Dembinsky Photo Assoc. Inc.: 16

On the cover...

Front cover: This *red fox* has beautiful red fur.
Page 2: Foxes like this one are very curious.

Table of Contents

On a cold winter's night, you sit at the edge of a meadow. You bring your hand up to your mouth and breathe through your fingers. You make a noise that sounds like an injured rabbit. You make the noise again and then you sit and watch. Out of nowhere, an animal appears at the far end of the meadow. It looks around, and then it disappears again. What could this creature be? It's a fox!

What Do Foxes Look Like?

Foxes have triangle-shaped ears, pointed noses, and bushy tails. In fact, they look a lot like dogs. That is because foxes and dogs belong in the same animal group. They are both *canids* (KAY–nidz). Wolves and coyotes are canids, too.

All foxes are covered with fur. The color of a fox's fur is very important—it helps the fox hide! Many foxes are colored to look like the dirt and rocks they live by. This protective coloring is called **camouflage**. It makes the fox very hard to see.

This *cross fox* is watching over its surroundings. ⇒

Most foxes only have one color of camouflage. But the *arctic fox* is different. It can change colors! The arctic fox lives in snowy areas, so in winter it is white to blend in with the snow. But when the snow melts, the arctic fox must change its color to match the ground. During the late winter and spring, the fox's fur slowly changes color. By summertime, the arctic fox is brown or gray to match the ground.

Do All Foxes Look the Same?

There are about 21 different kinds of foxes. They come in many different sizes and colors. *Red foxes* are large. They have red fur and black legs. *Gray foxes* have short legs and gray fur. *Swift foxes* are small and have longer hair. *Kit foxes* are skinny and have fur-covered toes.

This *gray fox* is watching a small animal. ⇒

Where Do Foxes Live?

Foxes can be found in almost every area on Earth. The gray fox lives in jungles, deserts, and forests. The red fox can be found everywhere except in very hot or cold areas. The arctic fox lives only in the Far North.

No matter where foxes live, they all make **dens** to stay in. Dens provide a safe place for the foxes to rest, raise their babies, and escape from enemies. The dens also keep the foxes warm and dry when the weather is bad. Foxes make their dens in hollow logs, under big rocks, and under fallen trees. They even dig dens right in the hard ground.

' This den is surrounded by colorful flowers. ⇒

Foxes are **predators**, which means that they hunt other animals for food. The animals foxes eat are called their **prey**. Foxes are very good hunters. They have good eyesight and keen hearing. A fox often sneaks up on its prey by crawling on its belly. It must be very quiet and patient. When it gets close enough, the fox leaps out quickly. It pins its prey to the ground with its strong legs. Then it is time to eat!

Foxes are mostly **nocturnal** animals. That means they are active at night and sleep during the day. At night, the foxes' prey are active, too. If foxes hunted during the day, they would probably not find as much food to eat.

Sometimes a fox catches more food than it can eat. When this happens, it takes the extra food to a safe place and buries it. Some foxes bury their food right in the ground. Others cover it with sticks or leaves. By burying their food, the foxes make sure other animals will not try to steal it. When the fox is hungry again, it simply digs up its meal!

This gray fox is getting ready to bury its prey. ⇒

What Do Foxes Eat?

Foxes eat many kinds of food. Mice and rabbits are favorite foods for most foxes. They also eat insects, birds, and lizards. Sometimes, foxes even eat berries and other fruits.

Foxes are also **scavengers**. That means they will eat almost anything they find—even dead animals. Sometimes these dead animals, called **carrion**, can make other animals very sick. But not foxes! Carrion is good for them. And by eating carrion, foxes help keep the countryside clean.

⇐ This fox is eating carrion from a dead bird.

What Are Baby Foxes Like?

A male fox is called a **dog fox**. A female is called a **vixen**. During the late winter, a dog fox and a vixen mate. Then they look for a den that is safe and quiet. They line the den with grasses and leaves to make it warm and dry. When spring comes, the vixen gives birth to her babies, called **kits**. A vixen usually has about five kits at a time.

These fox kits are waiting for their mother to come back. ⇒

When fox kits are born, they cannot see. They are helpless and weak. For two months their only food is the milk the vixen makes inside her body. Slowly, the kits grow stronger. When they are about four months old, the vixen teaches them how to hunt on their own. By the end of the summer, the kits have grown big and strong. They leave the den and go out to live on their own.

How Do Foxes Talk to Each Other?

Foxes talk to each other in many different ways. They leave smells on trees, grasses, and rocks. They use their bodies and tails to show when they are happy, angry, or frightened. But the most important way foxes talk to each other is by using sounds.

Foxes can make many different sounds. Each sound means a different thing. Some sounds mean "Here I am!" Others say "Danger!" By barking, whining, yipping, and growling, foxes let each other know how they feel.

⇐ This arctic fox is tilting its head as it listens to other foxes.

Do Foxes Have Any Enemies?

Coyotes, eagles, and bobcats are all enemies of the fox. But the fox's most dangerous enemy is people. For hundreds of years, people have hunted and trapped foxes for their beautiful fur. Many farmers kill foxes that they think are pests. And sometimes people leave out poisons that foxes eat by mistake.

This red fox is standing in the sunshine. ⇒

People harm foxes in other ways, too. Building roads and houses destroys the areas where foxes live. And when we harm too many other animals such as mice and rabbits, the foxes that eat them are left without food. To save the fox, we must learn to be more careful. If we understand more about the helpful fox, this clever animal will be around for a long time to come.

Glossary

camouflage (KAM–uh–flazh)
Camouflage is coloring that helps an animal blend in with its surroundings. Foxes use camouflage to hide from their enemies and prey.

carrion (KA–ree–un)
Carrion is the remains of a dead animal. Foxes will eat carrion if there is no other food to eat.

dens (DENZ)
A den is a fox's home. Foxes make their dens in hollow logs, under rocks, and even in the ground.

dog fox (DOG FOKS)
A dog fox is a male fox.

kits (KITS)
Kits are baby foxes. Kits live with their mothers for several months.

nocturnal (nok–TUR–null)
Nocturnal animals are active at night and sleep during the day. Foxes are nocturnal.

predator (PREH–duh–ter)
A predator is an animal that eats other animals. Foxes are predators.

prey (PRAY)
Prey is an animal that other animals hunt for food. Mice and rabbits are prey for foxes.

scavengers (SKA–ven–jerz)
Scavengers are animals that eat almost anything—even dead animals. Foxes are scavengers.

vixen (VIK–sen)
A vixen is a female fox.

Index